W9-CUR-800

COMMUNITY CONNECTIONS

?

PAPER BEADS FROM AFRICA
CHARITIES STARTED BY KIDS!
BY MELISSA SHERMAN PEARL

Published in the United States of America by Cherry Lake Publishing
Ann Arbor, Michigan
www.cherrylakepublishing.com

Reading Adviser: Marla Conn MS, Ed., Literacy specialist, Read-Ability, Inc.

Photo Credits: © Photo used with permission from PAPERbeadsFROMafrica, cover, 5, 9, 11, 13, 15, 17, 19, 21; © Photo used with permission from FUNDaFIELD, 7,

LIBRARY OF CONGRESS CATALOGING-IN-PUBLICATION DATA
Names: Pearl, Melissa Sherman, author.
Title: Paper beads from Africa : charities started by kids! / by: Melissa Sherman Pearl.
Other titles: How do they help?
Description: Ann Arbor : Cherry Lake Publishing, 2018. |
Series: How do they help?
Identifiers: LCCN 2017031848 | ISBN 9781534107311 (hbk) |
    ISBN 9781534109292 (pdf) | ISBN 9781534108301 (pbk) |
    ISBN 9781534120280 (hosted ebook)
Subjects: LCSH: Women refugees—Uganda—Juvenile literature. |
    Beadwork—Uganda—Juvenile literature. | Charities—Uganda—Juvenile literature.
Classification: LCC HV640.4.U33 P43 2018 | DDC 362.839814096761—dc23
LC record available at https://lccn.loc.gov/2017031848

Cherry Lake Publishing would like to acknowledge the work of The Partnership for 21st Century Learning. Please visit www.p21.org for more information.

Printed in the United States of America
Corporate Graphics Inc.

PAPER BEADS FROM AFRICA

CONTENTS

HOW DO THEY HELP?

GROWING UP HELPING OTHERS

The East African country of Uganda has had a long history of conflict and violence. In 1991, a **warlord** named Joseph Kony invaded northern Uganda. Many innocent people fled their villages. Children caught in this conflict have continued to suffer over the years in many ways.

In 2006, Kyle and Garret Weiss met Angolan kids impacted by war.

Two million people were displaced during the Kony war.

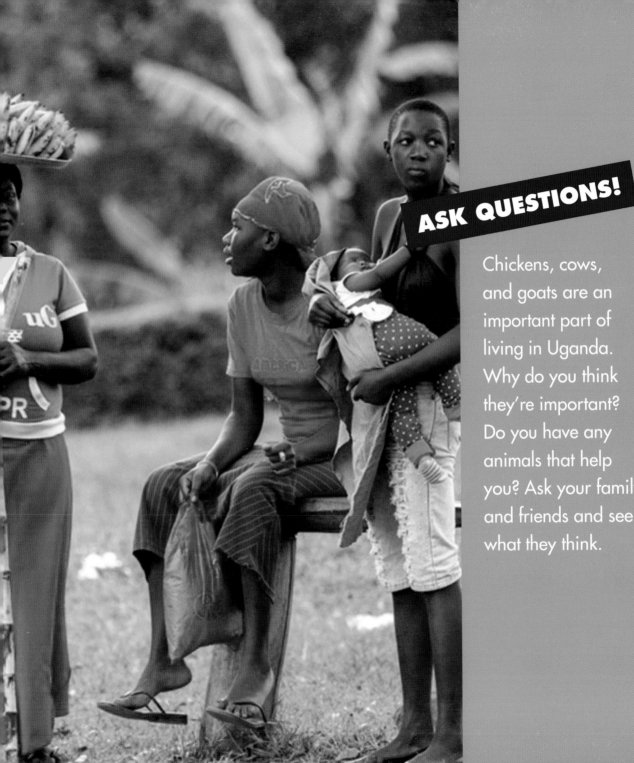

ASK QUESTIONS!

Chickens, cows, and goats are an important part of living in Uganda. Why do you think they're important? Do you have any animals that help you? Ask your family and friends and see what they think.

They learned that soccer was one of the greatest joys for many African kids who didn't have money to pay for equipment or fields. So the Weisses founded a charity called FUNDaFIELD. Weiss family vacations began to be spent in places like South Africa and Uganda. The boys' sister, Kira, also went along.

In 2010, while helping with a Ugandan soccer tournament, 12-year-old Kira discovered and fell in

FUNDaFIELD has created 11 soccer fields in 4 countries in Africa.

love with the local paper bead jewelry that was being sold there. Handmade by different women's groups, it was colorful and interesting—made from newspaper, calendars, and magazines. She brought some jewelry home and her friends loved it, too!

Paper beads are created by wrapping thin strips of paper around a dowel.

THINK!

Kira and her friends sold beads in front of coffee shops, at gift shows and holiday boutiques, and through small retail stores. Where do you think would be the best place to sell items to raise money?

9

THE VALUE OF PAPER BEADS

As Kira got to know the local women, she learned about making the beads. She also discovered that for many women, selling the beads was their only way of supporting themselves and their families. Kira started PAPERbeadsFROMafrica to aid these women.

During her next Uganda trip, Kira met women who were **refugees**

Uganda is in sub-Saharan Africa. That means it is south of the Saharan desert.

from the Kony war. They lived in Acholi Quarter, an IDP (**internally displaced person**) camp, and worked in a rock **quarry**. The work was physically difficult, and the **wages** were tiny. But the women were also learning and mastering the art of making the beautiful paper beads. Kira offered to pay them "fair trade" value for the beads—which was five times what they were earning at the rock quarry. Kira sold the jewelry back home and used the profits to help

Fair trade means those who produce goods in developing countries are paid a fair wage for their work.

Why do you think local bore holes (water wells) are an important part of life in Uganda? Because there is no indoor plumbing, the local bore holes are a source of water for the villagers. They use jerry cans to transport water to their homes for drinking, cooking, and cleaning.

13

in Uganda. Soon, the women could afford school uniforms and supplies for their kids' education.

The summer of 2014 brought devastating news to these women: the IDP camp would close. Once again these refugees would be homeless. Kira was determined to help these women who had already been through so much. But it was a big job. How would she move 31 women and 198 children?

Refugees are people forced to flee their home country. IDPs are people forced to flee their home, but who stay in their home country.

Kira and her friends launched a program called "Home by the Holidays." They continued selling the beads, but they also made a YouTube video and a CrowdRise fund-raising page. Their efforts allowed them to do more than just move the families. PAPERbeadsFROMafrica was able to build homes and donate farming tools, seeds, and everything the children needed for school.

But Kira and her team realized the women needed a **sustainable** future.

CrowdRise helps organizations raise money from people all over the world who want to help.

This led to the successful "After the Bulldozers" fund-raiser, which provided **livestock**, bikes, kitchen goods, comfortable sleeping mats, sheets, and blankets. It also allowed them to purchase jerry cans (to carry water) and **latrines** (community toilets) as the villages don't have indoor plumbing.

Some people have to walk miles to fill up their jerry cans with fresh water.

LOOK!

Many Ugandan families live in traditional mud and wattle huts. These homes have mud on the outside and thatched grass roofs. Look online or at the library to find out how they are made.

19

CREATIVE WORK

Now a college student, Kira still visits Uganda. She's thrilled about the women's thriving, sustainable lifestyle. Recently, new materials and jewelry-making techniques have been introduced, giving these women creative work that builds new skills as they supplement their income. And who doesn't love creative work that makes a difference? Kira does!

Farming and livestock affords the women's households plenty of food while selling excess produce at local markets makes money.

Do you have any old magazines or newspapers that aren't wanted and are ready to hit the recycle bin? Get crafty with it! You can make your own version of paper beads, collages, or maybe even hats.

GLOSSARY

internally displaced person (in-TUR-nuhl-ee dis-PLASED PUR-suhn) someone forced to flee his or her home but remaining within the country's border

latrine (luh-TREEN) a communal toilet, especially in camps or barracks

livestock (LIVE-stahk) farm animals that are raised, kept, and used by people

quarry (KWOR-ee) a large, deep pit from which stone or other material is or have been extracted

refugees (ref-yoo-JEEZ) people forced to leave their country to escape war, persecution, or natural disaster

sustainable (suh-STAY-nuh-buhl) meeting the needs of the present while preserving and helping the future

wages (WAYJ-ez) money paid to employees for the work they perform

warlord (WOR-lord) a military commander who exercises power by force, usually in a limited area

FIND OUT MORE

WEB SITES

www.paperbeadsfromafrica.com
Learn more about Kira's charity and the handcrafted paper jewelry.

www.fundafield.org
Learn more about FUNDaFIELD and what it does.

https://kidsunite4hope.org
Kids Unite 4 Hope was founded in 2015 by three siblings after a trip to volunteer with refugees in Turkey. The charity helps support these displaced children and families.

INDEX

ABOUT THE AUTHOR

Melissa Sherman Pearl is a mother of two girls who understands and appreciates that you don't have to be an adult to make a difference.